The Unofficial
Fantastic Beasts and Where to Find Them
Location Guide

B.L. Barreras
and
L.R. Barreras

©2016 B.L. Barreras and L.R. Barreras

Character names, films and books mentioned herein are the copyrighted property of their respective owners. This book is unofficial and unauthorized. It is not authorized, approved, licensed or endorsed by J.K. Rowling, her publishers, Warner Bros. or the creators of, or anyone otherwise associated with, *Fantastic Beasts and Where to Find Them* (or any of their related properties).

All rights reserved. No part of this book may be reproduced, in any form or by any means without permission in writing from the author.

Printed in the United States of America

First printing

This book is dedicated to my daughter and co-author, London - the biggest Harry Potter fan I know (and without whose help this book wouldn't have been finished) - and to my wife, Rebecca, and my son, Andrew, all of whom support me in everything I do.

TABLE OF CONTENTS

About This Book	5
How This Book Works	6
Chapter One: *FANTASTIC BEASTS* LOCATIONS IN NEW YORK CITY	8
Statue of Liberty	9
Ellis Island	11
Woolworth Building	13
Central Park - Gapstow Bridge	15
Central Park Zoo	17
Times Square	19
City Hall Subway Station	21
Chapter Two: NEW YORK CITY LOCATIONS THAT INSPIRED *FANTASTIC BEASTS* LOCATIONS	24
New York County National Bank	25
Tenement Museum	27
Adams Express Building	29
Writers House	31
Diamond District	33
124 Old Rabbit Club	35
Bill's Place	37
Bergdorf Goodman	39
Lower East Side	41
Chapter Three: NEW YORK CITY LOCATIONS THAT INSPIRED THE LOOK AND FEEL OF *FANTASTIC BEASTS*	44
Flatiron Building	45
New York Public Library	47
The Knickerbocker Hotel	49
Jefferson Market Library	51
Washington Square Park	53

Chapter Four: **56**
OTHER *FANTASTIC BEASTS* AND/OR HARRY POTTER
RELATED THINGS TO SEE AND DO IN NEW YORK CITY

Alice Tully Hall	57
Hogshead Tavern	58
Lyric Theatre	59
Watson Scavenger Hunts	60
Trivia, AD	60
The Group That Shall Not Be Named	60

Chapter Five: **62**
SUGGESTED ITINERARIES

Half-Day Itineraries: Downtown	63
Half-Day Itineraries: The Village and Chelsea	64
Half-Day Itineraries: Midtown and Central Park Area	65
Half-Day Itineraries: Midtown South	66
Themed Itinerary: Follow the Niffler	67
Full-Day+ Itineraries	68

Acknowledgements	**70**
Image Credits	**72**
Source Credits	**74**
Index	**76**
About the Authors	**79**
Help with this Book and Ordering Additional Guides	**80**

ABOUT THIS BOOK

This book's primary purpose is to provide additional information about the New York City locations where the events depicted in *Fantastic Beasts and Where to Find Them* would have occurred. I debated long and hard (with myself, which surprisingly weren't entirely one-sided debates) whether to write this book from the perspective of a No-Maj writing about the wizarding world (and treating the film as a kind of documentary) or as a wizard writing about wizarding history, but for No-Majs. However, in doing the research for this book, I discovered that there is an incredibly vast trove of information out there along these lines, and much of it is very well done (both the "official" information coming from J.K. Rowling as well as the information on various fan sites). Also, consistent with my other location guide (tied to the Broadway show *Hamilton*), this book is less a history book and more a travel guide to help fans of the film (and the world of Harry Potter generally) visit sites that have a connection with the film, and to learn about that connection and the history of the sites. We still tried to have fun with the book by connecting it as much as we could with the film, and we hope fans of the film appreciate what we have put together.

With this in mind, we have tried our best to explain how each location is used in *Fantastic Beasts*, either as a setting for a scene in the movie or as inspiration for a specific setting or the general look and feel of NYC in 1926. Hopefully, you will have the opportunity to see the movie and can use this book as a resource to help you learn about these locations or as a guide so that you can visit some of these locations and try to walk in the footsteps of the great wizards (and the pawsteps of the incredible beasts) that lived these tremendous adventures.

Because the wizarding world has been such a positive experience for me and my family, no less than 25% of any profits from sales of this book will be donated to charity, including HeForShe (it's a great cause, and my daughter loves Emma Watson).

 @BeastLocations

HOW THIS BOOK WORKS

We have tried to make this book as straightforward as possible, but a few things would benefit from explanation. A few different descriptions are used when referring to the characters, beasts and locations, with the following meanings:

- **Setting for** – this means the location is the setting in the film for the described events (although no filming was done in New York City, where a real New York location was used as that same location in the film, the location is considered the setting for purposes of this book);
- **Inspiration for** – this means the location was the inspiration for a specific location/setting in the film, or for the general look and feel of a portion of the film;
- **Who was there?** – this refers to which wizards or principal No-Majs appeared at that location in the film;
- **Which beasts were there?** – this refers to which beasts appeared at that location in the film. This does not include beasts that were in Newt's case when the case was at a location - the beast had to appear outside of the case to be included here (mostly);
- **Can you go there?** – this simply means whether the location stills exists in some form that might make it worth your while to see.

We would love any input, and if this book ends up seeing a lot of use we may prepare future updates or an expanded edition (especially if we get a lot of input from readers of this book). Please send suggestions or comments (e.g., locations to add, wizards or beasts we may have missed, or corrections) to blb@beastlocations.com, or tweet suggestions and include @BeastLocations. **Please also see page 80 for info on ordering additional paperback books – they make great gifts and stocking stuffers.**

If you like this book, it would mean a lot to us if you would share it on social media on Facebook, Instagram, Twitter, etc. – please include @BeastLocations and/or #BeastLocations.

ENJOY!

CHAPTER ONE

FANTASTIC BEASTS LOCATIONS IN NEW YORK CITY

New York City in 1926 was the setting for *Fantastic Beasts*, and many of the locations where events from *Fantastic Beasts* occurred are actual locations that existed in 1926 and that you can still visit today.

STATUE OF LIBERTY

Statue of Liberty and Bedloe's Island, 1927

Setting for: *The movie begins with Newt Scamander arriving into New York City on a ship, sailing in New York Harbor past the Statue of Liberty.*

Who was there? Newt Scamander

Which beasts were there? Demiguise (he's still in the case, but Newt talks to him)

Location: Liberty Island (ferry from Battery Park)

Subway: 🔴1 South Ferry; 🟢4 🟢5 Bowling Green
🟡R Whitehall Street/South Ferry

Can you go there? Yes – Statue of Liberty National Monument is open 9:30-3:30 every day but Christmas (see www.nps.gov/stli for hours during your visit). The island can only be reached by Statue Cruises ferry, and visiting the pedestal/museum or the crown require tickets that typically must be purchased in advance (statuecruises.com or (877) 523-9849). For a low-cost option, take a round-trip on the free Staten Island Ferry from Battery Park Ferry Terminal - you get a great view of the statue from the harbor.

Designations: U.S. National Monument (1924)
New York City Landmark (1976)
National Register of Historic Places (1966)
UNESCO World Heritage Site (1984)

No-Maj History/Items of Interest:

The Statue of Liberty (called "Liberty Enlightening the World") was designed by the French sculptor Frédéric Auguste Bartholdi and largely built by Gustave Eiffel (yes, the Eiffel Tower guy).

Bartholdi's earliest model was made in 1870, though the statue was not completed until 1884. The statue's right arm was exhibited in Philadelphia at the Centennial Exhibition in 1876 (and then moved to Madison Square Park in New York, where it stayed until it was returned to France for completion of the statue).

Bedloe Island was chosen as the site for the statue, both because of its location (ships entering the harbor had to pass by) and because it was owned by the U.S. government (having been ceded by New York state). Fort Wood (an army base used as a recruiting station during the Civil War) would be the site of the statue's foundation.

The statue arrived in New York in June 1885 and was greeted by 200,000 people lining the docks. However, efforts in the United States to raise the funds to build the statue's pedestal were largely unsuccessful, causing redesigns (to save money) and delays in construction. Thanks to the efforts of Joseph Pulitzer and the *New York World* (a NY newspaper) to raise $100,000 for the pedestal (with most donations being less than $1), the pedestal was finally completed in April 1886. Installation immediately began, and the 151-foot tall statue was dedicated on October 28, 1886.

Unsuccessful as a lighthouse (due to its faint light), the statue was transferred to the War Department in 1901 and eventually to the National Park Service in 1933. The island was renamed Liberty Island in 1956.

ELLIS ISLAND

Ellis Island Immigration Station, 1905

Setting for: *Newt Scamander disembarks and has to clear customs before being able to enter New York - this would typically have occurred on Ellis Island in the 1920s.*

Who was there? Newt Scamander

Which beasts were there? None

Location: Ellis Island (ferry from Battery Park)

Subway: 🔴 South Ferry; 🟢 4 🟢 5 Bowling Green
🟡 R Whitehall Street/South Ferry

Can you go there? Yes – Ellis Island is part of Statue of Liberty National Monument and is open 9:30-3:30 every day but Christmas (see www.nps.gov/stli for hours during your visit). The island can only be reached from New York City by Statue Cruises ferry (statuecruises.com or (877) 523-9849), and there is a bridge and a ferry from New Jersey. Ellis Island is included in all Statue of Liberty tickets, but there is a separate Hard Hat Tour that requires a special ticket.

Designations: U.S. National Monument (1965)
New York City Landmark (1993)
National Register of Historic Places (1966)
New Jersey Register of Historic Places (1971)

No-Maj History/Items of Interest:

One of the islands given the name Oyster Islands (due to the nearby oyster beds), the island was acquired by Samuel Ellis in the late 18th century and takes its name from him. It was acquired by the United States government in 1808.

The island was fortified and served as a federal arsenal from 1808 until 1814, and it remained a military post until becoming the first federal immigration station. The station opened on January 1, 1892, and processed over 400,000 immigrants during its first year. The present main structure opened in December 1900 (the original station was destroyed in a fire in 1897), and served as the immigration station until it was closed in November 1954 - it is estimated that 12 million immigrants were processed on Ellis Island.

The station remained unused until it became part of Statue of Liberty National Monument in 1965, and after a significant restoration the building reopened in September 1990 as the Ellis Island Immigration Museum (it was renamed the Ellis Island National Museum of Immigration in 2015).

The island itself has been expanded through landfilling several times over the years, with almost 90% of the island being part of New Jersey and the remaining portion (including the original island) being part of New York. Many of the buildings on the island remain abandoned and closed to the general public, though there are ongoing efforts to renovate more of these buildings (and the Ellis Island Hospital is now open for guided tours).

WOOLWORTH BUILDING

Setting for: *Headquarters of the Magical Congress of the United States of America (MACUSA), where Newt Scamander is initially taken by Tina Goldstein and which is later the site for Newt, Tina and Jacob Kowalski's escape from custody.*

Who was there?	Queenie Goldstein	Tina Goldstein
	Percival Graves	Jacob Kowalski
	Newt Scamander	Seraphina Picquery
Which beasts were there?	Bowtruckle	Obscurus
	Swooping Evil	
Location:	233 Broadway	
Subway:	1 2 3 A C J Z Chambers Street	
	4 5 6 Brooklyn Bridge – City Hall	
	R City Hall	
Can you go there?	Yes and no – you can visit and walk around the building, but unless you are a tenant or resident you can only visit inside by taking a tour (woolworthtours.com). Public tours are available every day at 2:00 (with two additional times on Saturdays), and private tours can be arranged.	
Designations:	National Historic Landmark (1966)	
	New York City Landmark (1983)	
	National Register of Historic Places (1966)	

No-Maj History/Items of Interest:

Frank Woolworth commissioned then-renowned architect Cass Gilbert to design the neo-Gothic style Woolworth Building as his corporate headquarters. The building was completed in 1912 and passed the Metropolitan Life Insurance Tower as the world's tallest building, a title it would hold until 1930 (when it was passed by 40 Wall Street; shortly thereafter both buildings were passed by the Chrysler Building, which withheld the placement of its now-iconic spire until 40 Wall Street was completed, so that it could claim the title). The Woolworth Building also had the world's fastest elevators, was the first office tower to include shops open to the public and was essentially fireproof, being faced with almost 2,000,000 terracotta blocks.

The F.W. Woolworth Company owned the building until 1998, although the company maintained a presence in the building through a Foot Locker store (Foot Locker is a successor to the F.W. Woolworth Company), though this connection is now gone.

The building was closed to the public for security reasons shortly after the September 11, 2001 attacks on the World Trade Center and was not reopened to the public (via tours given by Woolworth Tours) in 2014. Try to find the owl if you visit the building.

The top 29 floors of the building are being converted into luxury residences (including a seven level penthouse). Tenants in the building over the years have included Columbia Records, several Fordham University schools and a New York University school.

CENTRAL PARK - GAPSTOW BRIDGE

View of the Pond and the Plaza from Gapstow Bridge

Setting for: *Central Park scene, where we first see the Erumpent underneath the ice on the pond, with the bridge in the background, and then Newt Scamander and Jacob Kowalski pass an ostrich on the bridge. Finally, Tina Goldstein traps Newt and Jacob in Newt's case underneath the bridge.*

Who was there?	Tina Goldstein Jacob Kowalski Newt Scamander
Which beasts were there?	Erumpent
Location:	Crossing over the Pond, in the southeast section of Central Park (around 62nd Street, between 5th and 6th Avenues)
Subway:	N R W 5th Avenue/59th Street F 57th Street 4 5 6 59th Street/Lexington Avenue
Can you go there?	Yes - Central Park is open 365 days a year. The Park opens at 6:00AM and closes at 1:00AM, though you will have to consider your own level of comfort in visiting the Park at night. The bridge is about a quarter-mile walk from The Plaza (on Central Park South) and is located near Wollman Rink and the Central Park Zoo - visit www.centralparknyc.org and search for "Gapstow Bridge" for more information.

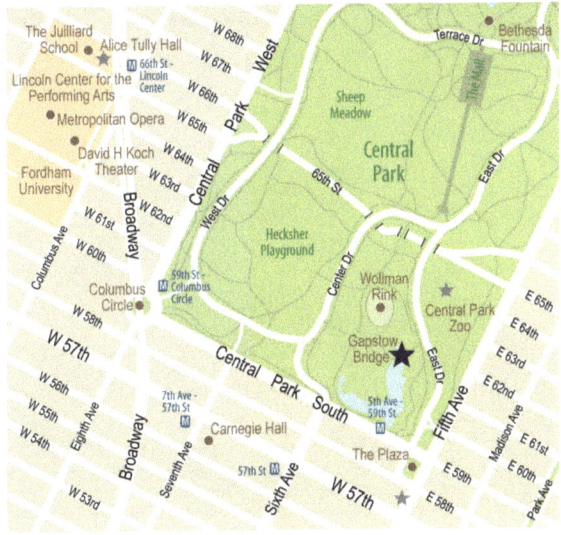

No-Maj History/Items of Interest:

Gapstow Bridge was originally designed by Jacob Wrey Mould in 1874 as a wooden bridge with elaborate cast iron railings. The original bridge deteriorated under excessive wear and was replaced by the current stone bridge, designed by Howard & Caudwell, in 1896. The bridge crosses the neck of the Pond and connects the Hallett Nature Sanctuary with the area by the Central Park Zoo.

In addition to being photogenic itself, the bridge also offers views of the Pond and the surrounding areas of the Park, as well as the city skyscrapers beyond. The skaters at Wollman Rink can be seen during the winter, and the Victorian Gardens Amusement Park (on the same site) can be seen during the warmer months.

The Pond is one of the seven naturalistic water bodies in Central Park and provides an area to find solitude and a break from the bustle of the New York City streets (though just a short distance away). The Pond is smaller than it once was, giving some of its area over to Wollman Rink, which opened in 1949.

The Hallett Nature Sanctuary is a fenced-in enclosure containing a 3.5-acre ecosystem that mimics the wild and to provides a secluded habitat for small animals and birds. The Central Park Conservancy offers guided tours of the Hallett and hosts periodic open hours from April through November - visit www.centralparknyc.org for more information. You can also hear a brief audiocast description of the Pond, the Hallett and Gapstow Bridge by Sarah Jessica Parker on the same website (search for "The Pond").

CENTRAL PARK ZOO

The Delacorte Clock at the Central Park Zoo

Setting for: *Central Park scene, where Newt Scamander and Jacob Kowalski find the Erumpent (near a very scared hippopotamus). Newt seduces (with a mating ritual) and almost captures the Erumpent in the zoo, though it ends up chasing Jacob out of the zoo and into Central Park.*

Who was there?	Jacob Kowalski Newt Scamander
Which beasts were there?	Erumpent
Location:	In the southeast section of Central Park (along 5th Avenue just inside the Park, at 64th Street)
Subway:	N R W 5th Avenue/59th Street F Lexington Avenue/63rd Street 4 5 6 59th Street/Lexington Avenue
Can you go there?	Yes - the Central Park Zoo is open 365 days a year from 10:00AM to 5:00 or 5:30 (4:30 in the late fall and winter) - visit centralparkzoo.com for exact hours, and note that the last entry is 30 minutes before closing time. The zoo is about a quarter-mile walk from the Plaza (on Central Park South) and is located near Wollman Rink. There is a fee for anyone over the age of 2.

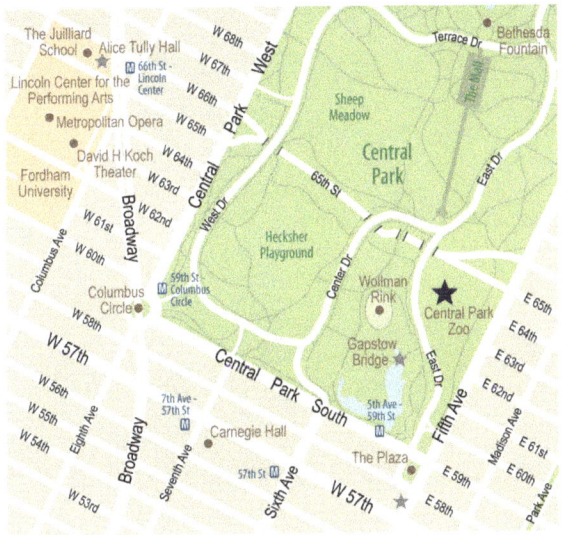

No-Maj History/Items of Interest:

The Central Park Zoo began as a menagerie near the Arsenal, originally housing exotic pets and other animals given to Central Park. A zoo charter was granted in 1864, and the zoo was permanently quartered behind the Arsenal in 1875.

Buildings to more properly house the zoo were built in 1934, and the Children's Zoo, which includes a petting zoo, was opened in 1961 (now the Tisch Children's Zoo). After years of deterioration, the zoo was closed in 1983. After five years of renovation and redesign, including the installation of more naturalistic enclosures, the zoo reopened in the summer of 1988. The zoo has been managed by the Wildlife Conservation Society since 1980.

Do not miss the George Delacorte Musical Clock located between the main zoo and the Children's Zoo (and be sure to hang around to see the figures on the clock move around to music, every half hour - during the winter holiday season the music takes on a holiday theme).

Possible the most famous zoo inhabitants were two polar bears, Gus and Ida - the polar bears are no longer at the zoo, both having passed away (Gus, who lived at the zoo from its reopening in 1988, was the last to survive, passing away in 2013).

In addition to *Fantastic Beasts*, the zoo has been featured in several films over the years, including the *Madagascar* animated films and *Mr. Popper's Penguins* (where it was also featured in the book).

TIMES SQUARE

Setting for: *A scene of destruction, as the Obscurus moves through the city creating chaos and destroying buildings following Percival Graves' betrayal of Credence Barebone. Tina Goldstein battles Graves so that Newt Scamander can go after the Obscurus.*

Who was there?	Credence Barebone Tina Goldstein Percival Graves Newt Scamander
Which beasts were there?	Obscurus
Location:	Times Square
Subway:	❶ ❷ ❸ ❼ Times Square – 42nd Street Ⓝ Ⓠ Ⓡ Ⓢ Times Square – 42nd Street Ⓐ Ⓒ Ⓔ 42nd Street – Port Authority
Can you go there?	Yes - Times Square remains a vibrant neighborhood and "The Crossroads of the World". Times Square is one of the most visited tourist attractions in the world, and in addition to the Broadway theater district and the street performers for which it is famous, it is surrounded by restaurants, shops and other tourist attractions.

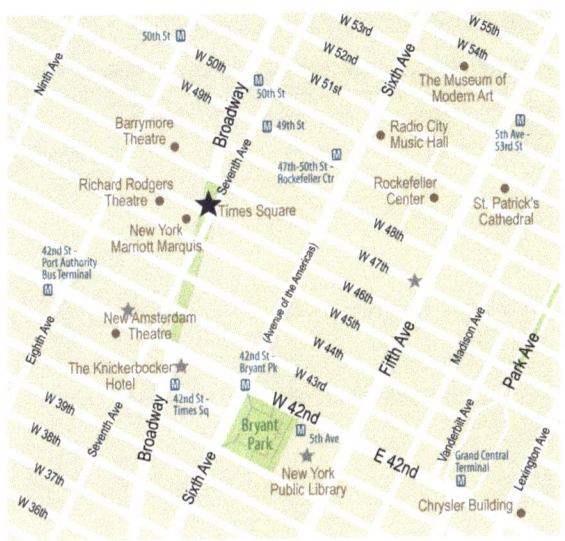

No-Maj History/Items of Interest:

Times Square was largely owned by successive individuals in the 18th and 19th centuries (including John Jacob Astor, who made a fortune dividing the area and selling lots to hotels and other businesses as the city spread uptown in the early 19th century). It was named Longacre Square in the late 19th century after London's Long Acre. By the 1890s the once-quiet area was home to theaters, restaurants and crowds of people.

The area was renamed "Times Square" after publisher Adolph Ochs moved his newspaper - the New York Times - to a new skyscraper on 42nd Street in 1904. The newspaper eventually moved, but the building, now known as One Times Square, remains famous as the site of the annual ball drop every New Year's Eve - 1 million people annually crowd the area for the drop.

Times Square has gone through several iterations over the years. After World War I it was a hub of theaters, music venues and hotels, but it was also known as a site for crime, gambling and prostitution (and this was furthered during the Great Depression, when Times Square became known as seedy, corrupt and dangerous, a reputation it would keep until the 1990s). Victory in Europe Day was celebrated by a massive crowd in Times Square on May 8, 1945. Times Square underwent massive renovations in the 1990s to change its image, including increased security, the closing of certain businesses (and the opening of others), and these efforts were continued in the 2000s with a ban on smoking and the closing of much of the square to create a pedestrian plaza.

CITY HALL SUBWAY STATION

City Hall Station, early 1900s

Setting for: *The final battle of the film - the Obscurus is followed into the subway station by pretty much everyone, and there is a terrific battle among the Obscurus, Percival Graves, Newt Scamander and Seraphina Picquery's aurors.*

Who was there?	Credence Barebone	Queenie Goldstein
	Tina Goldstein	Percival Graves
	Gellert Grindelwald	Jacob Kowalski
	Seraphina Picquery	Newt Scamander
	Henry Shaw, Sr.	
Which beasts were there?	Obscurus	Swooping Evil
	Thunderbird	
Location:	City Hall Park	
Subway:	① ② ③ Ⓐ Ⓒ Ⓙ Ⓩ Chambers Street ④ ⑤ ⑥ Brooklyn Bridge – City Hall Ⓡ City Hall	
Can you go there?	Yes, but only if you are a member of the New York Transit Museum - members can take a tour of the station (apparently these tours are hard to come by and sell out quickly). As a cheaper and quicker alternative, you can remain on the downtown 6 train as it loops over to go uptown (it passes through City Hall station).	
Designations:	National Register of Historic Places	

No-Maj History/Items of Interest:

City Hall Station opened to the public in October 1904, and the very first subway ride in New York City left from the station (the station was the southern end of the Manhattan Main Line). It was designed by renowned architects Heins & LaFarge to be the showpiece of the new subway system, and featured skylights, chandeliers and vaulted tile ceilings designed by Rafael Guastavino. Construction for the station and subway began in 1900, and you can still see a plaque commemorating the groundbreaking (in front of City Hall).

City Hall Station was built on a tight curve, and as ridership increased longer trains were put into service. The station was not able to accommodate the longer trains (which also now had center doors that opened far away from the platform), and it was also not an especially busy station, with the nearby Brooklyn Bridge station serving much more of the area transit needs. As a result, the city decided to close City Hall Station, and its final day of service was the last day of 1945.

The track remains active as a turnaround for the 6 line (as it turns from downtown to uptown service at Brooklyn Bridge station) - the station was also known early on as the "City Hall Loop" for this reason. If you stay on the train during this turnaround, you can catch glimpses of City Hall Station.

Plans to reopen the station as part of the New York Transit Museum were abandoned for security reasons, although the station was opened for the Centennial Celebration of the subway in 2004 and members of the Transit Museum can take guided tours.

CHAPTER TWO

NEW YORK CITY LOCATIONS THAT INSPIRED *FANTASTIC BEASTS* LOCATIONS

The following New York City locations were not featured in the film, but locations in the film were inspired by and sometimes based upon these locations.

NEW YORK COUNTY NATIONAL BANK

Inspiration for: ***Steen National Bank***, *where Jacob Kowalski tries (unsuccessfully) to get a loan to open up his bakery and meets Newt Scamander (who has his hands full trying to track down and capture his Niffler). This is also where we first meet Tina Goldstein, initially in front of the bank (listening to Mary Lou Barebone of the Second Salemers), who later takes Newt into custody outside the bank.*

Who was there?	Credence Barebone Mary Lou Barebone Tina Goldstein Jacob Kowalski Newt Scamander
Which beasts were there?	Bowtruckle Niffler Occamy
Location:	300 West 14th Street
Subway:	Ⓐ Ⓒ Ⓔ Ⓛ 14th Street ① ② ③ Ⓕ Ⓜ 14th Street
Can you go there?	Yes – the bank building remains there and is still an impressive site (though it no longer operates as a bank).
Designations:	New York City Landmark (1988)

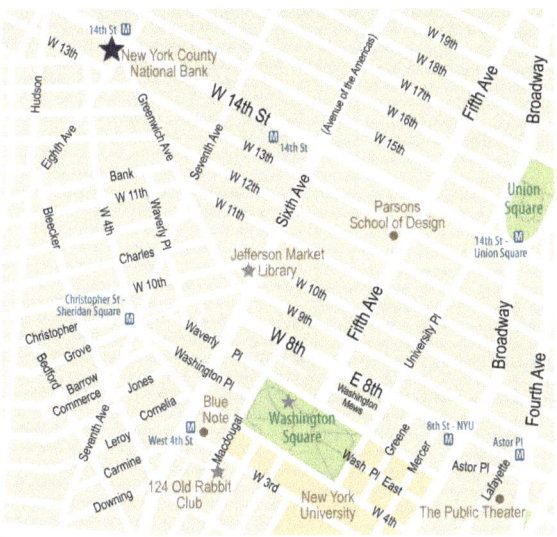

No-Maj History/Items of Interest:

The New York County National Bank was founded in 1855. After almost folding in 1902 (when its reserves were essentially gone), the bank recovered well enough to commission a new building for its headquarters, and the board selected the architectural firm De Lemos & Cordes for the project. The architect on the project was Rudolph L. Daus, who designed a neo-classical temple with Beaux-arts stylings, including massive Corinthian columns for the entranceway. Four arched windows on the 14th Street side of the building match the entrance. The building was completed in 1907.

Francis Leland, the president of the bank, died in 1916, and the bank was taken over five years later, by the Chatham and Phoenix National Bank. In 1926, it merged with the Metropolitan Trust Company. A few years later, it became a takeover target for Manufacturers Trust Company and was later renamed Manufacturers Hanover Trust Company in the mid 1960s. Manufacturers Hanover Trust operated a branch bank in the building until they merged with Chemical Bank in 1994, after which the building was no longer used as a bank (it remained empty for some time after the 1994 merger, although it saw a brief life as a theater).

The building was eventually converted to different usage in 1999, and is now in use as luxury residential apartments (and the original antique steel vault remains visible in the lobby).

TENEMENT MUSEUM

Inspiration for: *Jacob Kowalski's Apartment, where Newt Scamander's case is disastrously opened wide, allowing several beasts to escape (including a Murtlap, who attacks Jacob). Newt arrives on the scene first and uses a Repairing Charm on the apartment before Tina Goldstein can see what happened.*

Who was there?	Tina Goldstein Jacob Kowalski Newt Scamander
Which beasts were there?	Billywig Demiguise Erumpent Murtlap Niffler Occamy
Location:	97 and 103 Orchard Street
Subway:	🟠 Delancey Street ⚫⚫⚫ Essex Street 🟠🟠 Grand Street
Can you go there?	Yes – the Tenement Museum has a visitor center and shop that are open every day (except some holidays) from 10-6:30 (8:30 on Thurs), and runs tours of the tenement building at 97 Orchard St. (see tenement.org for more info and to book a tour).
Designations:	National Historic Site (1998) National Historic Landmark (1994) National Register of Historic Places (1992)

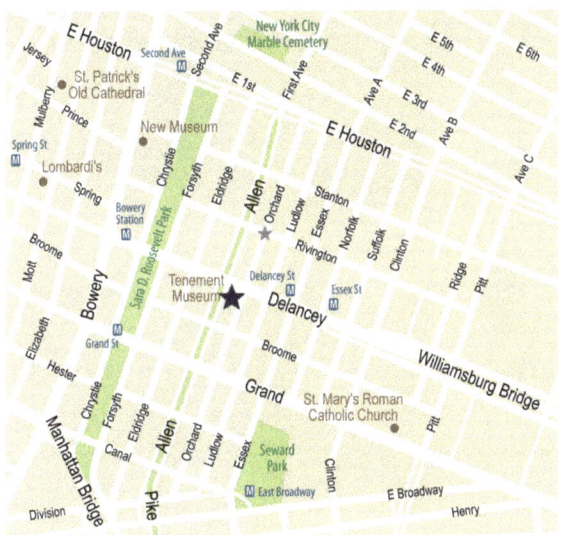

No-Maj History/Items of Interest:

The Tenement Museum consists of two buildings - the one housing the museum shop, classrooms and offices and 97 Orchard Street. This history is for 97 Orchard Street.

97 Orchard Street was built in 1863 and contained 22 apartments, as well as a saloon in the basement, and had no indoor plumbing or electricity. Over time more space was converted to commercial use, and electricity and indoor plumbing were installed. In 1935 the landlord chose to evict all the residents (rather than make legally required modifications, keeping only the commercial spaces open. While in use as a residence (from 1863 until 1935), 97 Orchard Street housed almost 7000 working class immigrants.

When the landlord evicted the tenants in 1935, the upper floors were boarded and sealed, and the building remained that way until discovered in 1988. While the building had deteriorated over time, the residences looked and were furnished as they had been in 1935. Fortunately the folks that discovered the tenement were looking for a museum, and they painstakingly researched the building and its inhabitants, and they were able to restore the building so that its visitors can see how the building's inhabitants lived their lives.

If you decide to take one of the tours, ask if the tour includes the room set in the 1920s that the creators of *Fantastic Beasts* toured as inspiration for designing Jacob Kowalski's apartment.

ADAMS EXPRESS BUILDING

Inspiration for: *Henry Shaw, Sr.'s Media Headquarters*, where Langdon Shaw brings Mary Lou Barebone, Credence Barebone and some of the other Barebones to share their story with Shaw Sr., who has no interest in hearing Mary Lou's explanation about the strange happenings in the city. Senator Shaw, Shaw Sr.'s oldest so, is equally dismissive, calling the Barebones "freaks" and insulting Credence (which may come back to bite him...).

Who was there?	Credence Barebone Mary Lou Barebone Henry Shaw, Sr.
Which beasts were there?	None
Location:	61 Broadway
Subway:	① Ⓡ Ⓦ Rector Street ② ③ ④ ⑤ Wall Street Ⓙ Ⓩ Broad Street
Can you go there?	Yes and no – you can visit and walk around the building, but the Adams Express Building is an operating office building and is not open to the public (see 61broadwaynyc.com for more info).

No-Maj History/Items of Interest:

The Adams Express Building was designed by Francis Kimball and was met with resistance when construction began in 1912. It was one of many tall buildings going up in the Wall Street area at the time, which led to concerns about blocking sunlight and airspace (and which ultimately led to a setback requirement in a 1916 revised zoning code). Constructions of the Adams Express Building was completed in 1914, before the zoning changes could go into effect.

The Adams Express Building was one of the many buildings in lower Manhattan that were damaged in 1916 during the Black Tom explosion (an explosion of a munitions depot on Black Tom Island in New York Harbor - the depot was attacked in connection with World War I, as it was storing (for later delivery to the Allied forces) small arms and artillery ammunition). The explosion registered between 5.0 and 5.5 on the Richter scale and blew out about 300 of the Adams Express Building's windows - it also caused substantial damage to the Statue of Liberty, resulting in the arm and torch no longer being open to visitors.

WRITERS HOUSE

Inspiration for: *Tina and Queenie Goldstein's Apartment*, where Tina takes Jacob Kowalski and Newt Scamander to keep an eye on them while they figure out how to capture Newt's escaped beasts. Queenie magically makes a strudel, much to Jacob's delight, and Tina and Queenie are distressed to discover that Newt and Jacob didn't stay the night (despite making them cocoa!).

Who was there?	Queenie Goldstein Tina Goldstein Jacob Kowalski Newt Scamander
Which beasts were there?	None
Location:	21-23 West 26th Street
Subway:	① ⑥ Ⓡ Ⓦ 28th Street Ⓕ Ⓜ 23rd Street
Can you go there?	Yes – the buildings can be seen from the street (see writershouse.com for more info about the agency that owns the house).
Designations:	New York City Landmarks

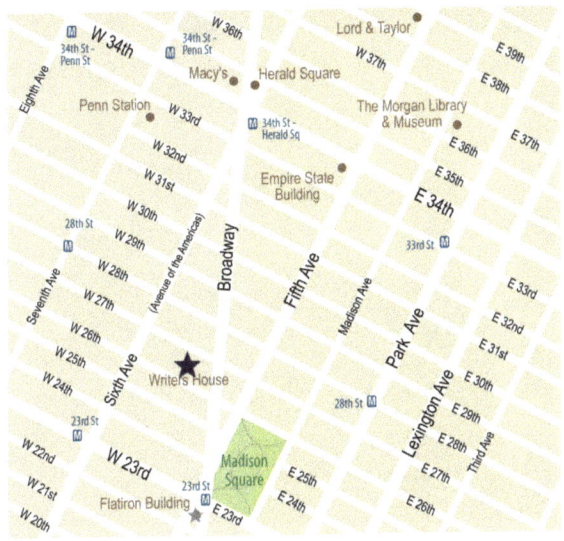

No-Maj History/Items of Interest:

Writers House consists of two adjacent buildings, both of which were built in 1881 by the brothers William Waldorf and John Jacob Astor III.

The buildings were acquired by Writers House (which is a literary agency) separately, 21 West 26th Street was acquired first, in 1979 (six years after the agency was founded).

23 West 26th Street was acquired more than 20 years later, and has a more colorful past. The building passed into the hands of the U.S. Communist party at one point. It was left by Vincent Astor to his daughter, and when her husband (a wealthy communist) died, it passed to the U.S. Communist party and served as the party's headquarters from the mid-1940s until the late 1950s. The Communist newspaper The Daily Worker was published from the house. The building was under surveillance by the FBI and was repeatedly firebombed while under Communist control.

One benefit from being constructed by two of the wealthiest men at the time is that each of the buildings contains concrete-lined vaults that are now used to store archival books by the agency's authors.

DIAMOND DISTRICT

Looking down 47th Street from Fifth Avenue - note the diamond-topped lampposts

Inspiration for: *Scene of Niffler's (second) capture, where Newt Scamander and Jacob Kowalski, on their way to Central Park, discover the Niffler inside a jewelry shop (despite the Niffler's ingenious attempt at camouflage), and Newt manages to capture the Niffler with an Accio spell after the two of them mostly destroy the shop. Jacob aids their escape from the police (despite the fact that he and Newt are covered in jewels) by pointing out an escaped lion.*

Who was there?	Jacob Kowalski Newt Scamander
Which beasts were there?	Niffler
Location:	47th Street, between Fifth and Sixth Avenues
Subway:	B D F M 47-50 Streets - Rockefeller Center 4 5 6 S Grand Central Terminal N Q R W 49th Street
Can you go there?	Yes – the Diamond District is a quintessential New York City place to visit, and there is a lot of fun window-shopping there.

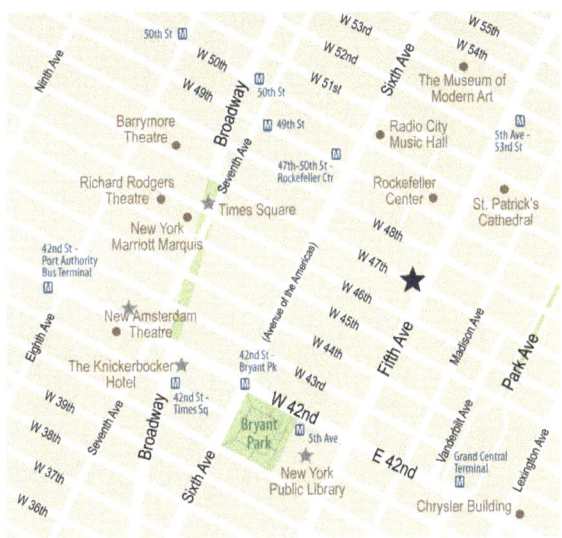

No-Maj History/Items of Interest:

The diamond districts in Manhattan moved north as the city and its residents expanded uptown. Diamond and jewelry dealers have congregated together at least since the 18th century, when there was a diamond district in lower Manhattan. Other early diamond districts were located in the Financial District and near Canal Street and the Bowery, both in the early 1900s (and one of these three areas is where the diamond district would have been located in 1926).

The move uptown began around 1941 and was precipitated at least in part by World War II as many in the diamond business fled Europe to settle in New York City. The primary diamond district in New York City has remained in mid-town ever since.

New York City's diamond district is a key part of the global diamond industry and is one of the largest and oldest diamond and jewelry districts in the U.S. (and only Jewelers' Row in Philadelphia has been around longer). New York City's diamond district remains important as the entry point for diamonds into the U.S. - almost 90% of all diamonds in the U.S. are estimated to come through New York.

Navigating through the diamond district is a different shopping (real or window) experience, as there are always salesmen out on the streets trying to drum up interest for the stores. The diamond business is also famous for finalizing deals with just a handshake.

124 OLD RABBIT CLUB

Below-grade entrance to 124 Old Rabbit Club

Inspiration for: *The entranceway to **the Blind Pig**, the speakeasy where Tina and Queenie Goldstein take Newt Scamander and Jacob Kowalski to see Gnarlak (to try to get information to help them find the Demiguise). After leading the group down a set of steps to a bricked up doorway, Tina and Queenie magically transform their outfits into 1920s flapper-style dresses (and Newt gives himself a tie). Tina knocks and a secret hatch opens up behind a poster, and the four of them are admitted into the speakeasy.*

Who was there?	Queenie Goldstein Tina Goldstein Jacob Kowalski Newt Scamander
Which beasts were there?	None
Location:	124 Macdougal Street
Subway:	Ⓐ Ⓒ Ⓔ Ⓑ Ⓓ Ⓕ Ⓜ West 4th Street ① Christopher Street - Sheridan Square ⑥ Bleecker Street
Can you go there?	Yes – 124 Old Rabbit Club is an active bar, open from 6:00PM until 2:00AM or 4:00AM (depending on the night).

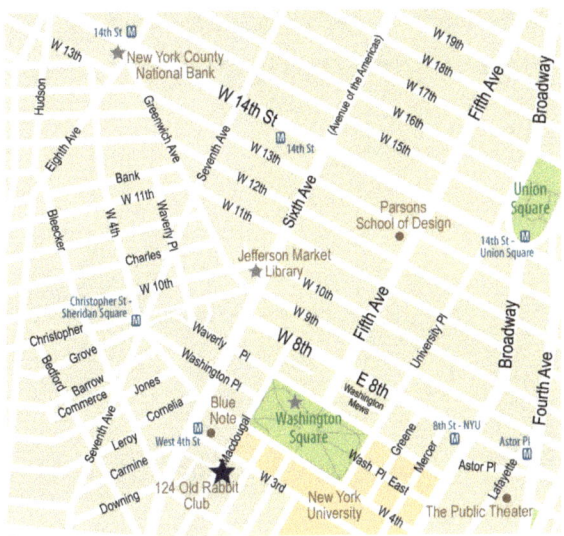

No-Maj History/Items of Interest:

Not a lot of historic information on 124 Old Rabbit Club...

From its unassuming and unmarked door to its location below street level (and posting its hours on the little mailbox on the wall to the right of the door), 124 Old Rabbit Club is a place you typically wouldn't just happen into - you need to be seeking it out (or be adventurous enough to follow the white rabbit into a dark place - think of Neo following the white rabbit to a club, which starts his adventure...).

Once you're inside (and it's small, dark and narrow, so expect to be close to your neighbors), it becomes clear that the specialty of the house is beer - the selection is much more diverse and eclectic than you might expect from such a small place. You can expect the bartender to know something about all the beers on the menu, so go with the vibe and order something you've never had.

While you're in front of the bar, take a look at the window and the door of the store to the immediate right, and see if you think the creators of *Fantastic Beasts* might have gotten some inspiration for the entranceway to the Blind Pig from the images on the window and door.

BILL'S PLACE

Inspiration for: *The interior of **the Blind Pig**, a speakeasy where Tina and Queenie Goldstein take Newt Scamander and Jacob Kowalski to see Gnarlak (to try to get information to help them find the Demiguise), and where Jacob tries his first shot of gigglewater. Gnarlak gives Newt some information (directing him to check out Macy's department store), but only after Newt hands over the Bowtruckle. Tina, Queenie, Newt and Jacob have to apparate away from the speakeasy to escape from MACUSA's aurors (who were apparently tipped off by Gnarlak).*

Who was there?	Queenie Goldstein Tina Goldstein Jacob Kowalski Newt Scamander
Which beasts were there?	Ashwinder (egg) Bowtruckle
Location:	148 West 133rd Street
Subway:	② ③ 135th Street Ⓐ Ⓑ Ⓒ 135th Street
Can you go there?	Yes – Bill's Place has jazz shows at 8:00PM and 10:00PM on Friday and Saturday nights; doors open at 7:30PM (call 212-281-0777 or see billsplaceharlem.com for reservations). Bill's Place does not serve alcohol.

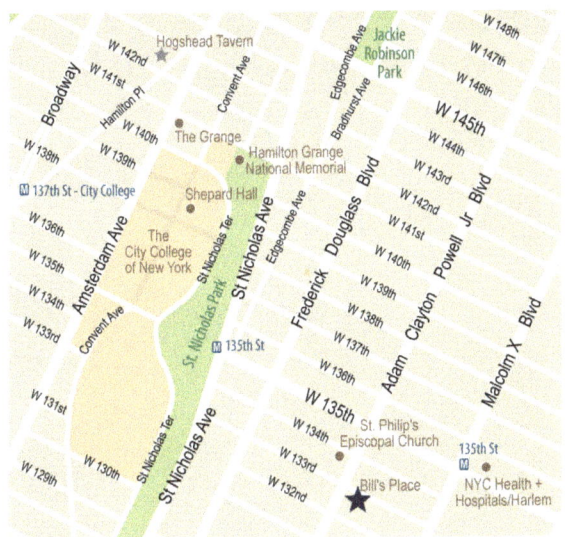

No-Maj History/Items of Interest:

Bill's Place calls itself Harlem's only authentic speakeasy and would have been around when *Fantastic Beasts* was set, getting its start during the 1920s (when Prohibition was just beginning) - the speakeasy is still located in its original location.

A number of famous jazz musicians have performed at Bill's Place over the years, and the plaque on the outside of the club proudly proclaims that Billie Holliday was discovered there in 1933. Holliday started singing in Harlem clubs as a teenager, starting a career that would span almost three decades and influence generations of jazz (and other) musicians. Holliday recorded a number of hits during her career, and her rendition of the popular jazz standard "Summertime" remains one of the best.

You can get a sense of being in an old speakeasy in the days of long-ago jazz by heading to the club, situated in a Harlem brownstone, on a Friday or Saturday night to listen to legendary jazz saxophonist Bill Saxton (this is the Bill of "Bill's Place") lead his band, the Harlem All Stars, through a set - be sure to make a reservation.

BERGDORF GOODMAN

Inspiration for: *Scene of Occamy's capture,* where Newt Scamander, Tina and Queenie Goldstein and Jacob Kowalski spot the Demiguise, and Newt realizes why the Demiguise escaped. Newt, Tina, Queenie and Jacob all have to work together to trap the now-enormous Occamy inside a tiny teapot.

Who was there?	Queenie Goldstein	Tina Goldstein
	Jacob Kowalski	Newt Scamander
Which beasts were there?	Demiguise	
	Occamy	
Location:	754 Fifth Avenue	
Subway:	(N) (R) (W) 5th Avenue/59th Street	
	(F) 57th Street	
	(4) (5) (6) 59th Street/Lexington Avenue	
Can you go there?	Yes – Bergdorf Goodman is a high-end department store, with a women's store (which is the main store) and a men's store across Fifth Avenue from each other. Both stores are open every day (from 10-9 on weekdays, 10-8 on Sat and 11-7 on Sun).	

No-Maj History/Items of Interest:

The company began in 1899, but only became known as Bergdorf Goodman in 1901, when Edwin Goodman purchased an interest in the business from Herman Bergdorf. Goodman would later purchase the remainder of Bergdorf's interest in the business but keep the name the same.

The business started in Union Square and moved a couple of times before settling in its present locations on Fifth Avenue in 1928 (so it would not have been in its present location when the film was set in 1926, though it would still have been on Fifth Avenue, a few blocks to the south). Goodman shrewdly courted other businesses to share storefronts in the new building (and to provide rental revenue), and the store was successful enough during the Great Depression that he was able to acquire the entire block.

Following Goodman's death, his son took over the company and headed it for about two decades, overseeing various expansions (both in physical space and in the range of merchandise carried by the store) until he sold the company in 1972, ultimately leading to its current ownership as a subsidiary of Neiman Marcus. The men's store was moved to a separate location across Fifth Avenue in 1990.

Bergdorf Goodman is one of the many stores along Fifth Avenue that creates elaborate window displays during the winter holiday season.

LOWER EAST SIDE

Inspiration for: Setting for **Jacob Kowalski's Bakery Shop**, where the scene opens with a shot of the sign at the corner of Orchard and Rivington and moves to Jacob's shop. We see Jacob's beast-inspired baked goods and a crowd of people, before a beautiful woman walks in and grabs Jacob's attention (he seems to find her familiar, for some reason...).

Who was there?	Queenie Goldstein Jacob Kowalski
Which beasts were there?	Demiguise Erumpent Niffler (all as baked goods)
Location:	Roughly the area east of Bowery and between Houston Street and Canal Street
Subway:	**F** Delancey Street **M J Z** Essex Street **B D** Grand Street
Can you go there?	Yes – the Lower East Side is one of the oldest neighborhoods in the city and remains a vibrant cultural scene.
Designations:	National Historic District National Register of Historic Places (2000)

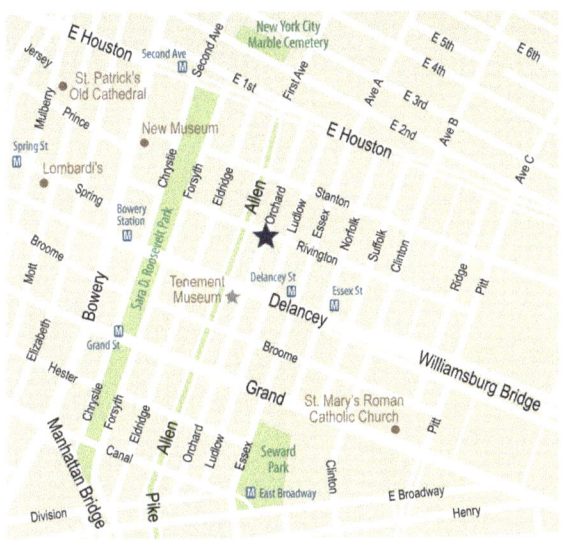

No-Maj History/Items of Interest:

Today the Lower East Side is bordered by Chinatown, Nolita and the East Village, but historically the Lower East Side included all of these neighborhoods, as well as Alphabet City, the Bowery and Little Italy (extending all the way to Broadway on the west and 14th Street on the north).

The majority of immigrants coming to New York City in the late 19th and early 20th centuries (primarily Europeans) settled in the Lower East Side and the crowded tenement buildings that were becoming prevalent there.

The neighborhood grew more diverse over the years (ethnically, politically and culturally). The Lower East Side became racially integrated with the influx of minority groups after World War II (a Spanish-speaking area known as Loisaida was primarily Puerto Rican). The East Village developed a separate identity when it became a popular destination for musicians and artists in the 1960s.

The popularity and gentrification of the East Village eventually spread to the Lower East Side (due to its proximity), turning it into a trendy neighborhood after years of decline, and it is now home to popular restaurants, upscale stores and luxury condominiums and hotels.

CHAPTER THREE

NEW YORK CITY LOCATIONS THAT INSPIRED THE LOOK AND FEEL OF *FANTASTIC BEASTS*

In creating the look and feel of New York City in 1926, *Fantastic Beasts* took inspiration from these five iconic buildings/areas of New York City, all of which existed at that time and convey the personality of the New York that the filmmakers wanted to portray. Where possible, images of these locations approximately as they would have looked in 1926 are included (along with a more recent image).

FLATIRON BUILDING

Flatiron Building, 1903

Location: 175 Fifth Avenue

Subway:  23rd Street

Visitor Info: The Flatiron Building is a working office building and not open to the public (though there are shops in the lobby that are).

Flatiron Building, 2016

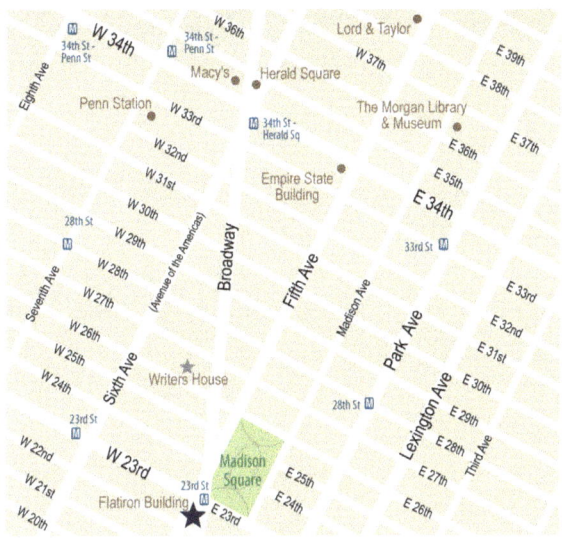

No-Maj History/Items of Interest:

The Flatiron Building was constructed in 1902 and was designed by Daniel Burnham, with Frederick Dinkelberg. It was among the early steel skeleton buildings in New York City (made possible by a change to the building codes in 1892 regarding the use of fireproofing materials). It was to be known as The Fuller Building (after architect George A. Fuller), but since it was constructed on a block already known as The Flat Iron the name stuck (it was also called Burnham's Folly, with many thinking the thin building would be knocked over by wind).

While it was never the tallest building in the world, the Flatiron Building quickly became a New York City icon, though it owed its popularity to the public (it was largely panned by the press and other critics). The building remained the primary iconic building in New York City until the construction of the Empire State Building in 1930.

The "cowcatcher" space at the front of the building was added to the design as retail space to produce revenue. This area is now known as the prow, and there are regular art exhibitions in the glass-enclosed space.

The Flatiron Building continues to be a commercial office building, but its purchase in 2009 by the Italian real estate firm Sorgente Group made lead to its eventual conversion to a luxury hotel (once the current tenant leases run their course).

NEW YORK PUBLIC LIBRARY

New York Public Library, 1908

Location: 476 Fifth Avenue

Subway: 🅑 🅓 🅕 🅜 42nd Street - Bryant Park
🟣7 5th Avenue
🟢4 🟢5 🟢6 🟣7 🅢 Grand Central Terminal

Visitor Info: The Main Branch of the New York Public Library is open from 10-6 Mon, Thurs-Sat, 10-8 Tues-Wed and 1-5 Sun.

Patience (dressed up for the holidays), in front of the New York Public Library, 2016

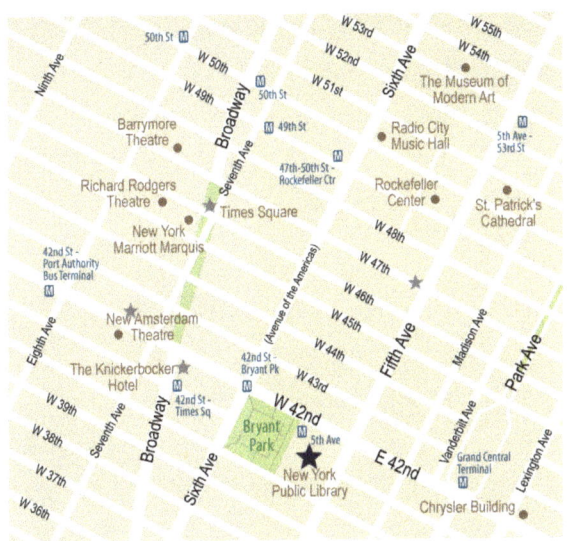

No-Maj History/Items of Interest:

Construction on the building to house the main branch of the New York Public Library was begun in 1902, and it was nine years later before the branch was officially opened in May 1911, with 75 miles of shelves and an initial collection of more than 1,000,000 volumes. At the time of its opening it was the largest marble structure in the U.S.

The collection of the library has grown over time and in the 1980s the library underwent an expansion that added more than 125,000 square feet (and which required the closing and excavation of adjacent Bryant Park, as the new library space was built underneath the park, which was restored above it).

The iconic lion statues at the front of the library facing Fifth Avenue - *Patience* and *Fortitude* - were created by E.C. Potter and the Piccirilli Brothers. The lions are often decorated with wreaths for the winter holidays.

Some of the library's more famous spaces, including the Rose Main Reading Room, are only accessible by the public through docent-led tours, which are available every day the library is open (though they are on a first come basis and limited in size; group tours are also available). The library also regularly houses exhibitions - see nypl.org for current listings (and be sure to look for the Stephen A. Schwarzman Building, which became the name for the main branch building following a donation to renovate the building's exterior, completed in February 2011).

THE KNICKERBOCKER HOTEL

The Knickerbocker Hotel, 1909

Location: 6 Times Square

Subway: ① ② ③ ⑦ Times Square – 42nd Street
Ⓝ Ⓠ Ⓡ Ⓢ Times Square – 42nd Street
Ⓐ Ⓒ Ⓔ 42nd Street – Port Authority

Visitor Info: The Knickerbocker Hotel is an operating hotel (theknickerbocker.com).

The Knickerbocker Hotel awning sign, 2016

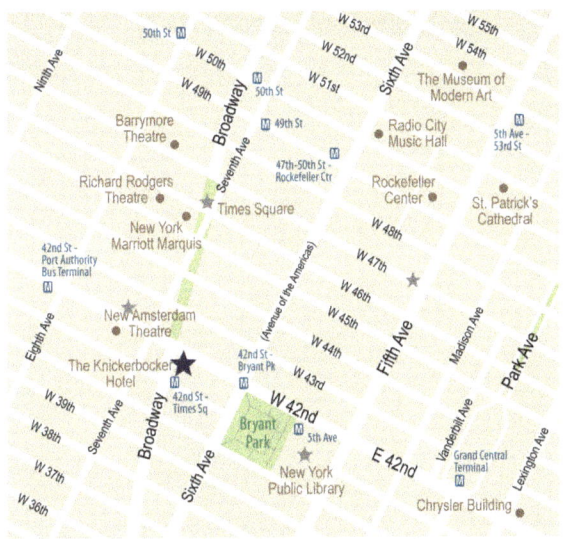

No-Maj History/Items of Interest:

The Knickerbocker Hotel opened in 1906 and was built by John Jacob Astor IV (who was a passenger on the Titanic's maiden voyage and did not survive) in the Beaux-Arts style. The luxurious building contained over 550 rooms and grand restaurants and bars on the lower three floors.

The hotel quickly became a key part of the New York social scene and helped transform Times Square into a vibrant tourist destination. Its legendary barroom became known as "The 42nd Street Country Club", and the martini is said to have been invented here (although this story has been disputed). Among others, Enrico Caruso, Charles Frohman and George M. Cohan were early longtime residents.

This popularity was not to last, however, as the onset of Prohibition eventually helped lead to the closing of the hotel in 1920. The hotel was converted to offices in 1920 (and renamed The Knickerbocker Building), and later became the home of *Newsweek* magazine, taking on the magazine's name.

After decades as an office building, the building was acquired by a real estate investment trust in 2012, completely gut-renovated (except for the landmarked exterior) and reopened as a hotel in 2015 under its original name. A scavenger hunt for you: an old sign for the hotel is posted over a doorway that used to connect the hotel to the subway (at the east end of the platform for the S subway).

JEFFERSON MARKET LIBRARY

Jefferson Market Library, 1935

Location: 425 Sixth Avenue

Subway: 🅐 🅒 🅔 🅑 🅓 🅕 🅜 West 4th Street
🅵 Christopher Street - Sheridan Square

Visitor Info: The Jefferson Market Library is open from 10-8 Mon-Thurs, 10-5 Fri-Sat and 1-5 Sun.

Jefferson Market Library, 2016

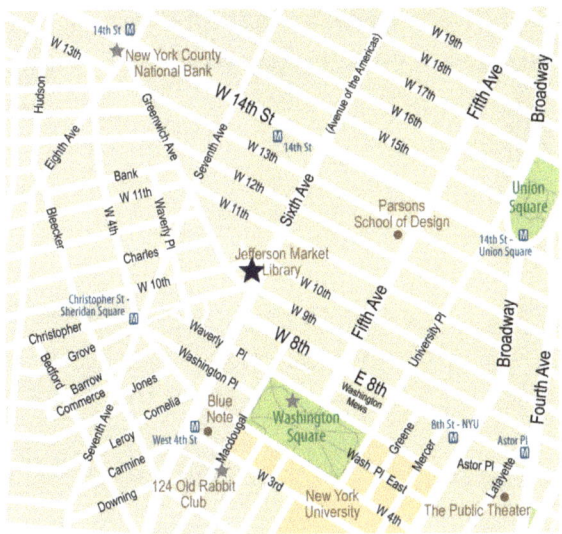

No-Maj History/Items of Interest:

The Jefferson Market Library building was commissioned as a courthouse and was designed by the firm Vaux and Withers. Completed in 1877, the building was seen as an architectural gem and was even voted one of the ten most beautiful buildings in America in the 1880s. The Jefferson Market, which stood on the site before construction of the building, was named after President Thomas Jefferson.

The courthouse was the site of several famous proceedings over the years, including the arraignment of the suspect in the murder of architect Stanford White in 1906 and the testimony of Stephen Crane (author of the Red Badge of Courage) in a proceeding in 1896.

While the building saw use as a courthouse for almost 70 years, redistricting led to the building ceasing to be a courthouse in 1945. It saw various agency uses in the following years (including as the Police Academy), but was ultimately left empty when the academy left in 1958.

Threatened with demolition, the building was saved by members of the community, and the mayor announced in 1961 that the building would become a public library. The conversion was undertaken by architect Giorgio Cavaglieri (who also converted the Astor Library into the Public Theatre) and completed in 1967. The building was listed on the National Register of Historic Places in 1972 and declared a National Historic Landmark in 1977.

WASHINGTON SQUARE PARK

Washington Square Park, 1936

Location: Greenwich Village (at Fifth Avenue, just south of 8th Street)

Subway: 🅐 🅒 🅔 🅑 🅓 🅕 🅜 West 4th Street
🅵 Christopher Street - Sheridan Square
🆁 🆆 8th Street - NYU

Visitor Info: Washington Square Park does not close.

Washington Square Park, 2016

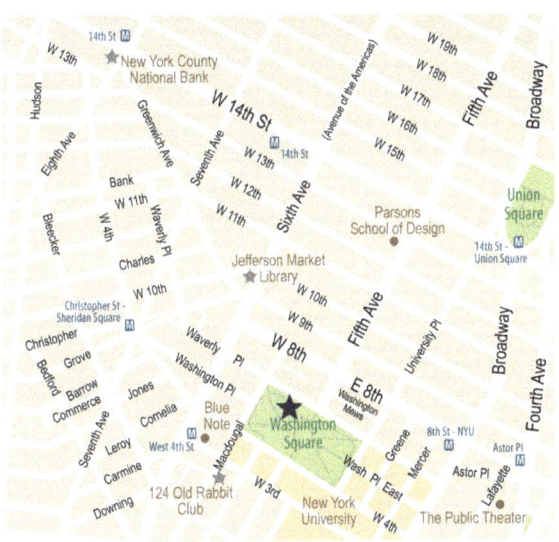

No-Maj History/Items of Interest:

After early uses as farmland and a public burial place, the land that would become Washington Square Park was purchased by New York City in 1826 and the Washington Military Parade Ground was created there (named after President George Washington).

Within just a few years, the area around the parade ground developed into a prime residential neighborhood (which it remains today).

The parade ground was redesigned several times into a park and came under the control of the NYC Department of Parks in 1871.

An arch was erected at the north end of the park in 1889 for the centennial celebration of Washington's inauguration as the U.S.'s first president. Originally constructed of plaster and wood, it was replaced with a marble arch designed by the architect Stanford White in 1892.

The park was redesigned yet again during Robert Moses' term as Parks Commissioner (which began in the 1930s). Fortunately Moses' plans to extend Fifth Avenue through the park met with opposition and were ultimately dropped (and the park was eventually closed to all auto traffic).

The park has a history of activist gatherings, protests and demonstrations and remains a popular gathering place for the community.

CHAPTER FOUR

OTHER *FANTASTIC BEASTS* AND/OR HARRY POTTER RELATED THINGS TO SEE AND DO IN NEW YORK CITY

There are a lot of other places or activities in the city that someone interested in *Fantastic Beasts* or Harry Potter generally may be interested in visiting or doing, even though they don't have any real connection with the New York City represented in the film. Some of them are listed in the following pages.

ALICE TULLY HALL

Location:	1941 Broadway
Subway:	❶ Ⓐ Ⓒ Ⓑ Ⓓ 59th St - Columbus Circle
	❶ 66th Street - Lincoln Center
	❶ ❷ ❸ 72nd Street
Visitor Info:	Alice Tully Hall is a venue for the performing and other arts and regularly hosts events. There is a stylish lounge facing Broadway where you can grab a drink (even if you are not attending a show at the hall).
Why go there?	Alice Tully Hall is a concert hall in the Julliard School Building, and is part of the Lincoln Center for the Performing Arts. It was the site of the world premiere of *Fantastic Beasts and Where to Find Them* on November 10, 2016, attended by the stars of the film and J.K. Rowling, among others.

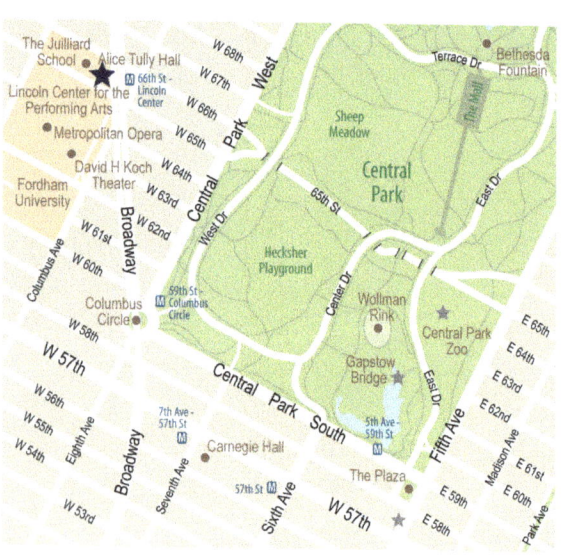

HOGSHEAD TAVERN

Location:	126 Hamilton Place (@143rd St.)
Subway:	① Ⓐ Ⓒ Ⓑ Ⓓ 145th Street
Visitor Info:	Hogshead Tavern is open 4:00PM-2:00AM and has Happy Hour Mon-Fri from 4:00-7:00 and brunch on Sat-Sun from 12:00PM-4:00.
Why go there?	It is not the Hog's Head Inn in Hogsmeade, but the tavern has a menu of delicious food and a great selection of craft beers. While they may not do it every year, the tavern was decorated in Harry Potter fashion for Halloween in 2016, with broomsticks and a sorting hat in the main room and Harry Potter-themed Wanted posters in the restroom.

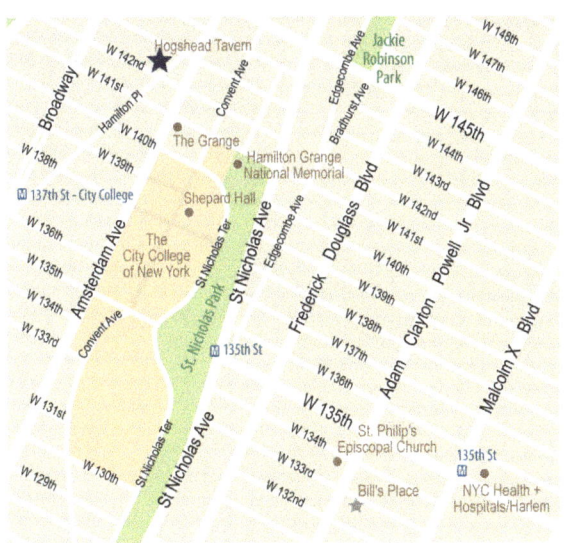

LYRIC THEATRE

Location: 213 W 42nd Street

Subway:
- ❶ ❷ ❸ ❼ Times Square – 42nd Street
- Ⓝ ⓠ Ⓡ Ⓢ Times Square – 42nd Street
- Ⓐ Ⓒ Ⓔ 42nd Street – Port Authority

Visitor Info: Lyric Theatre is an operating Broadway theater.

Why go there? Lyric Theatre may become more familiar to fans of Harry Potter in the near future, as it appears to be the venue for *Harry Potter and the Cursed Child* when it comes to Broadway in 2018. Showing the power of the Harry Potter franchise, the Lyric is reportedly closing its existing show early in order to get the *Cursed Child*.

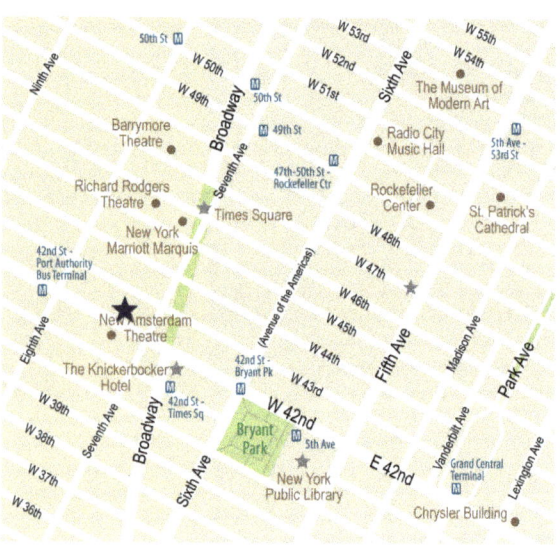

WATSON SCAVENGER HUNTS

What is this? Watson Adventures started in New York City and has been creating scavenger hunts since the early 1990s (they now have hunts in several cities). They have two Harry Potter-themed hunts: The Wizard School Scavenger Hunt (at the Metropolitan Museum of Art) and The Magical Creatures Scavenger Hunt (at the American Museum of Natural History).

Locations: Metropolitan Museum of Art
American Museum of Natural History

Visitor Info: Watson Adventures runs public hunts, private hunts and corporate events - see www.watsonadventures.com for more information and to book hunts.

TRIVIA, AD

What is this? Trivia, AD creates and hosts trivia events related to movies, television, books and pop culture, and they have two Harry Potter-themed trivia events: Harry Potter (Books) and Harry Potter (Movies). Trivia, AD typically award prizes to the team or individual that wins the event (but see their website for info about a specific event).

Locations: Various bars, pubs and taverns in New York and New Jersey

Visitor Info: Trivia, AD runs public trivia events and can arrange private and corporate trivia events - see triviaad.com for more information and to register for events. Events may only be for adults (they are held in bars), so please confirm before trying to register for a minor.

THE GROUP THAT SHALL NOT BE NAMED

What is this? We're not really sure. They call themselves the largest Harry Potter fan club in the world, but we haven't looked into them at all. Their website (meetup.com/tgtsnbn) does seem to list cool-sounding Harry Potter events, so you may want to check them out.

CHAPTER FIVE

SUGGESTED ITINERARIES

Now that you know where everything is, you need to figure out what you really want to see and whether you have time to see it. We have included some suggestions on the following pages, organized by the amount of time required (Half-Day or Full-Day+). We have also included a themed itinerary.

If you are planning your trip far enough in advance, you should think about booking a tour with On Location Tours, who teamed up with Warner Bros. Pictures to create a tour based upon *Fantastic Beasts* – given their relationship with Warner Bros. they should have all the inside scoop, and you can book the tour through onlocationtours.com (plus it's a bus tour, so you can cover a lot of ground).

Half-Day Itineraries

Downtown

Start by getting on the 6 train headed Downtown and stay on the train when it gets to the last stop, Brooklyn Bridge - City Hall; the train will loop through (1) *City Hall Subway Station* (page 21), and you can see the old station through the windows. Get off the train when it stops on the Uptown platform at the Brooklyn Bridge stop (DO NOT stay on - you will head back uptown!). A short walk across City Hall Park takes you to (2) the *Woolworth Building* (page 13), and around the corner from there you can get something to eat or a coffee at (3) the Woolworth Kitchen or Wooly Daily, respectively (Wooly Daily has old-time Woolworth Building postcards and cold-brewed coffee). From there head down Broadway to (4) the *Adams Express Building* (page 29) on your way to Battery Park for views of (5) the *Statue of Liberty* (page 9) and *Ellis Island* (page 11). If you have time, you can head to the Battery Park Ferry Terminal (see page 9) to take a round-trip on the free Staten Island Ferry to get a better view of the Statue of Liberty.

See the Full-Day+ Itineraries (page 68) if you're going to visit the Statue of Liberty and/or Ellis Island or if you're going to take a tour of the Woolworth Building as part of this itinerary (although you can probably squeeze a 30- or 60-minute Woolworth Building tour in and still do it in half a day - see page 13 for details).

Half-Day Itineraries

The Village and Chelsea

Start at (1) Macy's, which Gnarlak tells Newt to check out for something invisible (and where you can check out the windows if you're doing this around the winter holidays), and then swing by (2) *Writers House* (page 31) on your way to Madison Square Park, where you can take a break (and pick up a burger and a shake at Shake Shack if you're hungry) and get a great view of (3) the *Flatiron Building* (page 45). Next head south on Fifth Avenue, turn right on 14th Street and head to (4) *New York County National Bank* (page 25). Then walk southeast down Greenwich Avenue, past (5) *Jefferson Market Library* (page 51) and follow the map to (6) *Washington Square Park* (page 53) where you can take another break. Make your way to the southwest corner of the park and head south on Macdougal Street to (7) *124 Old Rabbit Club* (page 35), where you can reward yourself with a drink (if you're old enough and it's after 6:00PM, though I don't think you can order a shot of Gigglewater unless you're a wizard).

Note that this itinerary is about 2-1/2 miles from start to finish. If that's too far, you can save about a mile by taking the F/M subway downtown one stop from 6th/23rd (after (3) above), switching to the westbound L at 14th Street and taking it one stop.

Half-Day Itineraries

Midtown and Central Park Area

Start at (1) the *New York Public Library* (page 47) and head west along 42nd Street to (2) the ***Knickerbocker Hotel*** (page 49) and then north along Broadway to (3) ***Times Square*** (page 19), which is a good place to rest, grab a bite or just people-watch. From here you have a choice to get to (4) ***Alice Tully Hall*** (page 57): you can walk (about a mile) or take the 1 subway uptown from 42nd Street or 50th Street (depending where you are) to 66th Street. Lincoln Center is a nice place to wander around. Then head east on 65th Street (there's an entrance to Central Park on 65th) and make your way across the southern park of Central Park to (5) ***Gapstow Bridge*** (page 15) to (6) the ***Central Park Zoo*** (page 17). If you have time you may want to spend some time in the zoo, or just enjoy the area around the Pond (Gapstow Bridge crosses the Pond). Finally, you can see some of the big shops on Fifth Avenue as you make your way past Grand Army Plaza (cut out of the southeast corner of Central Park) and then down to (7) ***Bergdorf Goodman*** (page 39) - you'll pass the Apple Store and if you keep heading south past Bergdorf Goodman you'll pass Tiffany's, Henri Bendel and more (you have to go all the way to 50th to get to Saks Fifth Avenue).

Half-Day Itineraries

Midtown South

If you're staying around (1) *Times Square* (page 19), or just want to start there, you can head south to see several of the locations that inspired the look and feel of 1926 New York City for the film. Head south on Broadway to (2) the *Knickerbocker Hotel* (page 49), and then head east on 42nd Street (which gives you a great view of the Chrysler Building, as well as the Grace Building just north of Bryant Park) to (3) the *New York Public Library*, Main Branch (page 47). There are often special exhibits at the New York Public Library (and they are usually free), so you may want to pop inside. Walk back through Bryant Park (which is the site of an ice rink and shops during the winter holidays) to Sixth Avenue and then head south to (4) Macy's. After any shopping (window or real) there, head further south on Broadway and swing by (5) *Writers House* (page 31) on your way to Madison Square Park for a nice view of (6) the *Flatiron Building* (page 45), and you can take a break in the park and grab a burger and shake at the Shake Shack there (the original NYC location).

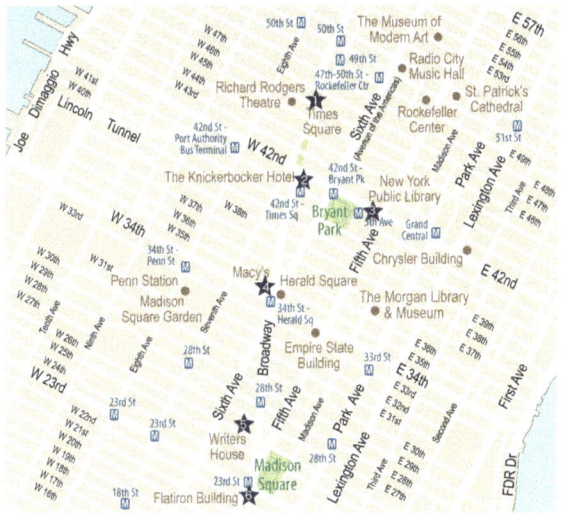

As with some of the other itineraries, this one involves a substantial amount of walking (about two miles), so keep this in mind from a timing and stamina perspective.

Themed Itinerary

Follow the Niffler

This itinerary will take you all over the city and will require a full day unless you skip some portions (I haven't in any way tried to make this itinerary move efficiently through the city - rather we follow the Niffler's path around the city from the film). Since this itinerary covers so much area, I decided not to include a map – go to the individual pages for location and subway information.

The Niffler first escapes from Newt Scamander's case when some coins on the steps of the *New York Country National Bank* (page 25) lure the Niffler out of the case. Unfortunately the Niffler is captured there by Newt and locked back in the case (after Newt makes the Niffler surrender the shiny booty).

Tina Goldstein takes Newt (and his case, with the Niffler inside) into custody outside the bank and escorts them to MACUSA headquarters at the *Woolworth Building* (page 13), where she opens the case to show the Niffler to Seraphina Picquery. Except the Niffler's not there because...

...Newt's case got switched with Jacob Kowalski's case at the bank, and Jacob took it home to the *Tenement Museum* (page 27). Newt and Tina make their way there, but not before the case gets opened and the Niffler escapes again. Tina takes Jacob and Newt back to her and Queenie Goldstein's place at *Writers House* (page 31) - the Niffler's not there, but it's their next stop to eat and rest before getting back on the Niffler's trail.

Newt thinks the Erumpent may be headed up to Central Park (based on Jacob's suggestion), so he and Jacob head north (after sneaking out on Tina and Queenie), and while they're walking through the *Diamond District* (page 33), something catches Newt's eye inside a jewelry shop... The Niffler is masterful at eluding Newt as they destroy the jewelry shop and is almost able to make a break for it when a crashing window sends Newt and the Niffler out of the shop, but a well-timed and aimed Accio spell by Newt leaves the Niffler stuck to a shop window, where Newt captures him yet again and locks him back in the case.

The last time we see the Niffler is in Jacob's bakery in the *Lower East Side* (page 41), and it's not really the Niffler that we see but rather one of Jacob's fantastical baked good creations in the shape of the Niffler.

Now that you've worked up an appetite, head over to Lombardi's (see the map on page 42) for the best white pizza in the city.

Full-Day+ Itineraries

If you have one or more full days, you can start to think about seeing most of the locations in this book and/or taking the tours offered at some of the locations. Each bullet point below should take about a day, so combine them if you have more time and want to see more.

- **Combinations of Half-Day Itineraries**

    You can combine any two of the half-day itineraries (pages 63-66). Note that these itineraries cover a lot of ground and involve a lot of walking, so make sure your whole group is up for it before you try to tackle two in one day.

- **Themed Itinerary**

    The Niffler-themed itinerary (page 67) should take most of a day, especially if you take one of the tours at the *Tenement Museum* (page 27).

- **Half-Day Itinerary plus Tour/Activity**

    Many of the half-day itineraries include one or more of the locations that offer a tour or further exploration that, depending on what you choose to do could, extend the itinerary to a full day. Examples for the different itineraries include:

    <u>Downtown</u> - visiting the *Statue of Liberty* (page 9) or *Ellis Island* (page 11), taking the *City Hall Subway Station* tour (page 21) (if you're a member of the New York Transit Museum) or taking the 90-minute *Woolworth Building* tour (page 13).

    <u>Midtown and Central Park Area</u> - visiting the *Central Park Zoo* (page 17) or the Hallett Nature Sanctuary (see page 16).

- **Adding a Scavenger Hunt or Trivia Event**

    If you're interested in a scavenger hunt or trivia event (see page 60 for both), you can combine these with an itinerary to make a full day out of it.

ACKNOWLEDGEMENTS

First and foremost, the inspiration for this book was clearly *Fantastic Beasts and Where to Find Them* (and, more broadly, the entire wizarding world of Harry Potter). J.K. Rowling is clearly the preeminent storyteller of our time, and she has created an entire exciting wizarding world that lives not in some far-off world or other dimension, but rather alongside our own mundane Muggle (or No-Maj) world, where we can almost touch it (or at least we can imagine we can). My family and I are incredibly thankful that we (or at least the kids) have grown up in a world with wizards, Muggles, No-Majs and fantastic beasts. Rowling has managed to craft story after story that not only has introduced millions of kids to a love of reading but that has also captured the imagination of just as many (if not more) adults. By not simplifying (or shortening) her books or characters to appeal to kids, she has introduced children to complex characters, storylines and themes while making the books compelling to her adult audience.

Almost equally important has been bringing the books to life in films, and the work there is equally amazing. We have had real (and many) conversations about which is better - a particular book or movie, and the arguments are often different scene by scene - and our views often change because the books and the films each are just as good (if not better) every time we see or read them. And here Rowling must share credit with the wonderful actors that have been tasked with bringing the world of Harry Potter to life - there really are too many amazing actors to name them all, and the quality has continued with the cast of *Fantastic Beasts*. Not to be dismissed are the examples that have been set in real life by these actors, many of whom have gone on to other successes and become leaders and role models for others, using their success and fame to further worthy causes.

Most important though is our family. Rebecca, wife and mom, continues to provide unwavering support for everything we do (even the crazy idea to write a book, now times two). Andrew was busy dancing this fall and winter, so London became co-author for this book (though this had as much to do with her obsession with and knowledge of everything Harry Potter). We are very lucky to have each other, and we are very happy that Harry Potter is a big part of our lives.

Thanks for everything – We couldn't have done this without you!

IMAGE CREDITS

All photographs included in this book were taken by me (using my iPhone 6-plus) except for the following photographs, drawings or paintings:

Cover, City Hall Station - By Unknown photographer [Public domain], via Wikimedia Commons [cropped by B.L. Barreras]

Page 9, Statue of Liberty - By Unknown photographer for Department of Agriculture [Public domain], via Wikimedia Commons

Page 11, Ellis Island - By A. Coeffler [Public domain], via Wikimedia Commons

Page 21, City Hall Station - By Unknown photographer [Public domain], via Wikimedia Commons

Page 45, Flatiron Building - By Unknown photographer [Public domain], via Wikimedia Commons

Page 47, New York Public Library - By Detroit Publishing Company (Library of Congress) [Public domain], via Wikimedia Commons

Page 49, Knickerbocker Hotel - By Unknown photographer [Public domain], via Wikimedia Commons

Page 51, Jefferson Market Library - By Berenice Abbott [Public domain], via Wikimedia Commons

Page 53, Washington Square - By New York Public Library (https://www.flickr.com/photos/nypl/3110612824/) [No restrictions], via Wikimedia Commons

All maps included in this book were created by Eureka Cartography (www.maps-eureka.com).

SOURCE CREDITS

Including source attributions throughout the book doesn't really fit well with the layout of the book (and this is more of a tour guidebook than a history book, though I did spend a lot of time getting the history part correct). So rather than fact-by-fact attribution, I would like to instead recognize the sources that I used for this book.

First and foremost was the film *Fantastic Beasts and Where to Find Them*, which we saw on opening weekend (of course)! It was while watching the film (the first time - both London and B.L. have seen the film multiple times) that the connection with New York sites became apparent, and subsequent viewings of the film were as much for research as for enjoyment.

The timing of publication of J.K. Rowling's screenplay of *Fantastic Beasts and Where to Find Them* was incredibly helpful in determining which characters and beasts were at which locations, as well as with the order of the locations in the film.

There was also an incredible amount of press around both the film and the connection with locations in New York City (so much so that it raised a question whether to do this book). These articles proved very helpful, as there was much discussion about the New York City locations that inspired different locations in the film (or the settings generally), and most of the identification in this book about locations that were inspirations for the film was based upon these various articles. Google Maps even now includes several of the settings from the film, and this was also helpful to this book.

Beyond the film and the screenplay, most research was done online and onsite. Where information about visiting a location was given, this information was taken as much as possible from the actual location (e.g., pamphlets or displays) or directly from the website for the location (and I similarly tried to take historical information directly from that location or website, though this was often not provided). The images other than my own photographs were primarily obtained through Wikimedia Commons, mainly because it was the most direct source of public domain images (due to the site's own guidelines for posting images on the site).

INDEX

124 Old Rabbit Club, 35, 36, 64
Adams Express Building, 29, 30, 63
Alice Tully Hall, 57, 65
Ashwinder, 37
Astor, John Jacob, 20
Astor, John Jacob III, 32
Astor, John Jacob IV, 50
Astor, Vincent, 32
Astor, William Waldorf, 32
Barebone, Credence, 19, 21, 25, 29
Barebone, Mary Lou, 25, 29
Bartholdi, Frédéric Auguste, 10
Bergdorf, Herman, 40
Bergdorf Goodman, 39, 40, 65
Billywig, 27
Bill's Place, 37, 38
Black Tom explosion, 30
Bowtruckle, 13, 25, 37
Bryant Park, 66
Central Park Zoo, 16, 17, 18, 65, 68
Chrysler Building, 14, 66
City Hall Park, 21, 63
City Hall Subway Station, 21, 22, 63, 68
Crane, Stephen, 52
Demiguise, 9, 27, 35, 37, 39, 41
Diamond District, 33, 34, 67
Eiffel, Gustave, 10
Ellis Island, 11, 12, 63, 68
Erumpent, 15, 17, 27, 41, 67
Flatiron Building, 45, 46, 64, 66
Gapstow Bridge, 15, 16, 17, 65
Gigglewater, 37, 64
Gilbert, Cass, 14
Gnarlak, 35, 37, 64
Goldstein, Queenie, 13, 21, 31, 35, 37, 39, 41, 67
Goldstein, Tina, 13, 15, 19, 21, 25, 27, 31, 35, 37, 39, 67
Goodman, Edwin, 40
Grand Army Plaza, 65
Graves, Percival, 13, 19, 21
Great Depression, 20, 40
Grindelwald, Gellert, 21
Hallett Nature Sanctuary, 16, 68
Hogshead Tavern, 58
Holliday, Billie, 38
Jefferson Market Library, 51, 52, 64
Knickerbocker Hotel, 49, 50, 65, 66

Kowalski, Jacob, 13, 15, 17, 21, 25, 27, 28, 31, 33, 35, 37, 39, 41, 67
Longacre Square, 20
Lower East Side, 41, 42, 67
Lyric Theatre, 59
Macy's, 37, 64, 66
Madison Square Park, 10, 64, 66
Moses, Robert, 54
Mould, Jacob Wrey, 16
Murtlap, 27
New York County National Bank, 25, 26, 64, 67
New York Public Library, 47, 48, 65, 66
Niffler, 25, 27, 33, 41, 67, 68
Obscurus, 13, 19, 21
Occamy, 25, 27, 39
Picquery, Seraphina, 13, 21, 67
Pond, The, 15, 16, 65
Potter, Harry, 56, 58, 59, 60
Prohibition, 38, 50
Pulitzer, Joseph, 10
Saxton, Bill, 38
Scamander, Newt, 9, 11, 13, 15, 17, 19, 21, 25, 27, 31, 33, 35, 37, 39, 67
Shake Shack, 64, 66
Shaw Sr., Henry, 21, 29
Staten Island Ferry, 9, 63
Statue of Liberty, 9, 10, 63, 68
Swooping Evil, 13, 21
Tenement Museum, 27, 28, 67, 68
The Group That Shall Not Be Named, 60
Thunderbird, 21
Times Square, 19, 20, 65, 66
Trivia, AD, 60, 68
Washington Square Park, 53, 54, 64
Watson Scavenger Hunts, 60, 68
White, Stanford, 52, 54
Wollman Rink, 15, 16, 17
Woolworth, Frank, 14
Woolworth Building, 13, 14, 63, 67, 68
Woolworth Kitchen, 63
Wooly Daily, 63
Writers House, 31, 32, 64, 66, 67

ABOUT THE AUTHORS

B.L. Barreras and L.R. Barreras are a father-daughter team, and this is their first work together.

ABOUT B.L.
This is the second Unofficial Location Guide written by B.L., following closely after his first book earlier in 2016 - *Where Was the Room Where It Happened?: The Unofficial* Hamilton - An American Musical *Location Guide*. Being a self-published author, B.L. made a lot of mistakes with his first book that he hopes made this second effort better (it definitely made it quicker). *Where Was the Room Where It Happened?* is now being carried in retail locations around New York City, as well as some locations in New Jersey, Philadelphia and at the National Archives museum shop in Washington, D.C. (and hopefully more by the time you're reading this), and it is available online where books are sold, in both ebook and paperback versions.

B.L. started his career as a mechanical engineer in Houston, TX, and relocated to Manhattan to attend law school at NYU. He has spent most of the past 20 years as a lawyer in New York City, though he has taken breaks both from being a lawyer and from living in New York (spending two years abroad, in London and Frankfurt). He lives on the Upper West Side in Manhattan with his wife of 24 years, his two kids and their Jack Russell terrier, and he serves on the board of the nearby Bloomingdale School of Music, which has been providing open access to music education for more than 50 years.

ABOUT L.R.
This is L.R.'s first book, and it fits in well with her passion for Harry Potter and the wizarding world. L.R. is a senior at the Bronx High School of Science, where she is the secretary of the Harry Potter Club (among other things). She is currently deep in the college application process and is waiting (as patiently as she can) to find out where she'll be spending the next four years of her life. She is literally a life-long Harry Potter fan, having been born (in London) a couple of years after the first book was published (and, yes, it was the UK version *Harry Potter and The Philosopher's Stone* that we read to her). She had a Harry Potter birthday party when she turned 11, has read all the books at least seven times each (some more), seen the movies not quite as many times, and absolutely adores Emma Watson.

L.R. is one of the two kids mentioned in B.L.'s bio above and lives in her "cave" downstairs (a big step up from a cupboard under the stairs).

HELP WITH THIS BOOK

We want to make this guidebook as accurate and useful as possible, and we very much welcome any help we can get from readers. If you spot any mistakes that you think need to be fixed or additions that you think should be included, please let us know. Also, if you're visiting any of the locations using this book, we would love to hear how you like the locations, whether you discover anything you think would be fun for others to know, or to see pictures of the locations!

Also, all feedback is appreciated, whether it's to let us know that you love the book or even to tell us what you don't like about it.

Feedback can be sent to blb@beastlocations.com, or you can tweet comments using @BeastLocations or #BeastLocations. And follow us:

 @BeastLocations

ORDERING ADDITIONAL GUIDES

Additional guides can be ordered online (Amazon or B&N) or purchased at retail locations (www.beastlocations.com will eventually have a list of locations). Email me at blb@beastlocations.com for bulk orders or to carry the book in your store. The book can also be customized (with your company color and/or logo on the cover) for corporate gifts - email me at blb@beastlocations.com for further information.

This book is also available as an eBook on Amazon. The eBook has hyper-links to navigate you through the book (and to external websites), as well as zoomable fonts, maps and pictures.

THANKS SO MUCH FOR READING OUR BOOK!